METRICS

By
STEVE DAVIS

COPYRIGHT © 1999 Mark Twain Media, Inc.

ISBN 1–58037–114–0

Printing No. CD-1340

Mark Twain Media, Inc., Publishers
Distributed by Carson-Dellosa Publishing Company, Inc.

Table of Contents

Introduction

For some reason, the term metrics has a negative connotation with Americans. However, we live with metrics in our lives each and every day. For over 20 years, America has been slowly moving toward the metric system. You can see metrics on a soda can, a bag of potato chips, the speedometer of your car, and many other places.

This book will guide you through how mankind first began to develop measurements and why there was a conversion to the metric system. Then you will be challenged to use the metric system. Once you use it and know how to make conversions, you will feel better about the metric system.

The activities vary from easy to difficult. The student can use an activity as either a refresher for better understanding or as a challenge activity.

centimeter   kilometer   gigaliter   milligram

g   nl   μm   Gg

dm   daG   Mm

NET WT. 13 OZ (369g)

Name: _____ Date: _____

History of Measurements

      Imagine yourself in ancient Greece, the Roman Empire or Mesopotamia. You have established a small community with several other family groups and are now ready to trade with neighboring communities for the goods your community cannot provide. How are you going to do this without knowing how to measure fluids, weights, or grains? To top all of this off, how do you know how much to pay for the goods if you cannot agree on a measurement?

      This has been a problem for many centuries. Each country or nation had established its own standard of measurement based primarily on what the ruler had decreed. When you wanted to trade outside of your country, you could expect that the other country would not be using your measurements, but a different standard instead.

      The smart businessman always wants to get the most for the least money. Without one standard for measuring goods, someone will always come away from a trade richer, and someone will come away poorer. What do you use to create a standard of measure? You could use a rock, but how do you make more rocks of the same weight? You could use your arm, but then someone else's arm would be smaller or longer than yours. To establish a standard of measure, you would choose items from your environment that could be recreated and copied without much difficulty. Think about these places and what you would use.

1. Think of yourself as an Eskimo. What do you use for a standard measure of length?

_____

    What about a standard for weight?

_____

    How about a standard measure for volume (liquids)?

_____

2. You are now on a tropical island. What do you use now for measuring length, weight, and volume?

_____

_____

_____

_____

_____

Name: _____ Date: _____

"Passus" Activity

Let's look at some older measures of length.

In Roman days, a mile was 1000 double steps or "mille passus." One double step, or "passus," was about five feet, or 1.52 meters. This means that a Roman mile was about 5000 feet, or 1520 meters.

Get a yardstick and a meter stick. Now have one of your classmates take two steps. Measure the length he or she went in those two steps. Repeat this for each student in the class and fill in the table below. You may need to make additional copies of the chart. Did everyone get five feet or 1.52 meters as the length of a double step? Why not?

Name	Feet	Meters

Add everyone's lengths together and then divide by the total number of students in the class. This will get you an average for a double step. Was the average closer to five feet?

	Feet	Meters
Total		
Average		

Name: _____ Date: _____

English Measurements

Eventually, the English converted the Roman mile to the distance of 5280 feet, which we use today. However, for many years their neighbors in Scotland and Ireland used 5940 feet for a Scottish mile and 6720 feet for an Irish mile.

The English were the first to attempt to standardize measures. Did you know that the Magna Carta (1215) was part of this attempt? In fact, at this time, the "Iron Yard of our Lord the King," or just the **yard**, was created. It was determined that a yard would be divided into three feet, with 12 inches in each foot. An inch at this time was measured by placing three barley corns end to end.

Here are some English measurement units:

    1 rope = 20 feet
    1 rod or pole = 5.5 yards
    40 rods = 1 furlong (originally this meant "furrow long")
    8 furlongs = 1 mile
    3 miles = 1 league
    1 acre = 40 square poles or rods (an early definition of an acre was the amount of
        land one yoke of oxen could plow in a day—that is difficult to put a number
        on, isn't it?)

Try These

1. Convert one furlong into yards, feet, and ropes.

_____

2. How many yards are in one league?

_____

3. How many ropes are in one mile?

_____

4. How many square yards, feet, and ropes are in an acre?

_____

5. Measure your classroom in feet and meters. Convert these measurements to ropes, and then to rods.

_____

Name: _____ Date: _____

Volume Activity

Finally, let's look at the differences in weights and **volumes** (or capacities) used prior to the metric system.

The **barrel** is a measure of volume or capacity used in all systems of early measure, and it is still used today.

British barrel = 36 gallons
U.S. petroleum barrel = 42 gallons
U.S. liquid barrel = 126 quarts = 31.5 gallons
U.S. dry barrel = 105 quarts = 26.25 gallons

Write a letter to your local water supply district and ask him or her to provide the dimensions of a water tower in your school district. Determine the volume of the water tower in both cubic feet and cubic inches. Convert these answers into U.S. liquid barrels by using 0.1337 cubic feet = 1 gallon and 231 cubic inches = 1 gallon. Finally convert the U.S. barrels into British barrels.

Cubic feet _____

Cubic inches _____

U.S. liquid barrels from cubic feet _____

U.S. liquid barrels from cubic inches _____

British barrels _____

5

Name: _____ Date: _____

Hundredweights

Consider the notion of a **ton** for weight. A British long ton equals 2240 pounds, while the U.S. short ton equals 2000 pounds. The reason for the difference lies in how **hundredweights** are measured.

In Britian, one hundredweight is four British quarters, or 112 pounds. Each British quarter equals two stones, and each stone equals 14 pounds.

In the United States, one hundredweight is four U.S. quarters, or 100 pounds. Each U.S. quarter equals 25 pounds.

1. Let's say you export 35 pick-up trucks overseas. Each truck weighs approximately 3500 pounds. How many British hundredweights is this? How many stones?

_____

2. How many U.S. hundredweights is this? How many quarters?

_____

History of Metrics

The following is a chronology of the SI *(Systéme International d'Unités)* Metric System provided by the U.S. Metric Association and maintained on Colorado State University's web page.

1670 - Authorities give credit to Gabriel Mouton, a French vicar, for originating the metric system.

1790 - Thomas Jefferson proposed a decimal-based measurement system for the United States. France's Louis XVI authorized scientific investigations aimed at a reform of French weights and measures. These investigations led to the development of the first "metric" system.

1792 - The U.S. Mint was formed to produce the world's first decimal currency (the U.S. dollar consisting of 100 cents.)

1795 - France officially adopted the metric system.

1812 - Napoleon temporarily suspended the compulsory provisions of the 1795 metric system adoption.

1840 - The metric system was reinstated as the compulsory system in France.

1866 - The use of the metric system was made legal (but not mandatory) in the United States by the *Metric Act of 1866* (Public Law 39-183.) This law also made it unlawful to refuse to trade or deal in metric quantities.

1875 - *Treaty of the Metre* was signed in Paris by 18 nations, including the United States. The treaty provided for improved metric weights and measures and the establishment of the General Conference on Weights and Measures (CGPM) devoted to international agreement on matters of weights and measures.

1889 - As a result of the *Treaty of the Metre*, the United States received a prototype meter and kilogram to be used as measurement standards.

1893 - These metric prototypes were declared "fundamental standards of length and mass" in the *Mendenhall Order.* Since that date, the yard, pound, etc. have been officially defined in terms of the metric system.

1916 - The Metric Association was formed as a non-profit organization advocating adoption of the metric system in U.S. commerce and education. The organizational name was later changed to the U.S. Metric Association (USMA.)

1954 - The International System of Units began its development of the 10th CGPM. Seven of the new metric base units were adopted.

1960 - The meter was redefined in terms of wavelengths of light by the 11th CGPM, and the new metric system was given the official symbol SI for the *Systéme International d'Unités,* the "modernized metric system."

1964 - The National Bureau of Standards (NBS) made the metric system its standard "except when the use of these units would obviously impair communications or reduce the usefulness of a report."

1968 - Public Law 90-472 authorized a three-year *U.S. Metric Study,* to determine the impact of increasing metric use on the United States. This study was carried out by the National Bureau of Standards (NBS).

1971 - The *U.S. Metric Study* resulted in a *Report to the Congress: A Metric America, A Decision Whose Time Has Come.* The report concluded that the United States should, indeed, "go metric" deliberately and carefully through a coordinated national program and establish a target date 10 years ahead, by which time the United States would be predominately metric.

1973 - The UCLA/USMA/LACES/STC and other professional groups' National Metric Conference, the largest ever held, with 1700 registrants, took place in Los Angeles in September. The American National Metric Council (ANMC) was formed as a not-for-profit, non-advocative trade organization to plan and coordinate SI implementation by U.S. industry.

1974 - The *Education Amendments of 1974* (Public Law 92-380) encouraged educational agencies and institutions to prepare students to use the metric system of measurement as part of the regular educational program.

1975 - The *Metric Conversion Act of 1975* (Public Law 94-168) was passed by Congress. The Act established the U.S. Metric Board to coordinate and plan the increasing use and voluntary conversion to the metric system. However, the Act was devoid of any target dates for metric conversion.

1979 - The Treasury Department's Bureau of Alcohol, Tobacco, and Firearms (BATF) required wine producers and importers to switch to metric bottles in seven standard (liter and milliliter) sizes.

1980 - The Treasury Department's Bureau of Alcohol, Tobacco, and Firearms (BATF) required distilled spirits (hard liquor) bottles to conform to the volume of one of six standard metric (liter and milliliter) sizes.

1982 - President Ronald Reagan disbanded the U.S. Metric Board and canceled its funding. Responsiblity for metric coordination was transferred to the Office of Metric Programs in the Department of Commerce.

1983 - The meter is redefined in terms of the speed of light by the 17th CGPM, resulting in better precision, but keeping its length the same.

1988 - The *Omnibus Trade and Competitiveness Act of 1988* amended and strengthened the Metric Conversion Act of 1975, designating the SI metric system as the preferred measurement system and requiring each federal agency to be metric by the end of fiscal year 1992.

1991 - President George Bush signed *Executive Order 12770, Metric Usage in Federal Government Programs* directing all executive departments and federal agencies to implement the use of the metric system.

1994 - The Fair Packaging and Labeling Act (FPLA) was amended by the Food and Drug Administration (FDA) to require the use of dual units (inch-pound and metric) on all consumer products.

1996 - All four Canadian Stock Exchanges began decimal trading on April 15, the first exchanges in North America to abandon the old "pieces-of-eight" trading system and welcome the new decimal system. The old tradition of trading stocks in increments of one-eighth of a dollar, or 12.5 cents, dates back to when the Spanish mille dollar divided into "pieces-of-eight."

2000 - All agreements, contracts, and plans processed by individual states for federally-funded highway construction must be in metric units. This deadline has been cancelled by recent Congressional action, leaving metric conversion as voluntary, but still recommended to comply with the *Omnibus Trade and Competitiveness Act of 1988*. The vast majority of the State Departments of Transportation are using the metric system now, and they plan to continue despite the deadline being rescinded.

2000 (or soon after) - U.S. Stock Exchanges change to decimal trading. As an intermediate step toward that goal, stock prices are now quoted in sixteenths, or 6.25 cent increments, down from eighths, or 12.5 cents. The switch to decimal trading will bring the United States in line with the rest of the world's major exchanges. This follows the change of the Canadian Stock Exchange to decimal trading in 1996.

2009 - All products sold in Europe (with limited exceptions) will be required to have only SI metric units on their labels. Dual labeling will not be permitted. The original deadline was 1999, but the *EU Commission* voted to extend the deadline for 10 years, giving more time for companies to comply and for the U.S. regulations to allow metric-only labeling on consumer products.

Name: _____ Date: _____

Metric Internet Rodeo #1

1. Go to **http://www.bipm.fr/enus/1_Convention/member_states.html** and list the 48 member nations of the *Convention of the Metre* (the replacement for the *Treaty of the Metre.*)

_____

_____

_____

_____

_____

_____

_____

2. Go to **http://www4.law.cornell.edu/uscode/15/205c.html** (the *Metric Conversion Act of 1975*) and explain what "hard-metric" means:

_____

_____

_____

3. Go to **http://www4.law.cornell.edu/uscode/15/205d.html** (the *Metric Conversion Act of 1975*) and list who the 17 members of the U.S. Metric Board are.

_____

_____

_____

_____

Name: _____ Date: _____

4. Go to **http://vm.cfsan.fda.gov/~dms/flg-3.html** *(Fair Packaging and Labeling Act)* and list the four proper examples of correct labeling according to the Food and Drug Administration.

_____

_____

_____

_____

_____

_____

_____

5. According to the FDA, what is included in the net quantity of contents statement?

_____

_____

_____

_____

6. According to the FDA, what is the policy on using qualifying phrases in net quality statements?

_____

_____

_____

_____

_____

Metric Symbols

Metric symbols will have two parts at most. The **stem** will consist of the actual unit name for the type of measurement used. The **prefix** will come before the stem, if it is used, and will describe how large the unit actually is.

Let's look at the stem, or unit, for each type of measurement:

Type of Measurement	Unit Name	Symbol
Length	meter	m
Mass/Weight	gram	g
Volume/Capacity	liter	L or l

The prefixes describe the size of the measurement and are listed below from largest to smallest (all possible prefixes are not listed):

Prefix Name	Symbol	Decimal Value	Fraction Value	Description
giga	G	1,000,000,000		billion
mega	M	1,000,000		million
kilo	k	1,000		thousand
hecto	h	100		hundred
deca or deka	da	10		ten
deci	d	.1	1/10	tenth
centi	c	.01	1/100	hundredth
milli	m	.001	1/1000	thousandth
micro	μ	.000 001	1/1,000,000	millionth
nano	n	.000 000 001	1/1,000,000,000	billionth

By placing the prefix name with the stem, you get the full description of the measurement. For example:

Prefix	Stem	Full Name	Description	Decimal Description	Equivalent Symbol
centi	+ meter =	centimeter =	a hundredth of a meter =	0.01 meter =	1 cm

Name: _____ Date: _____

Metric Prefix Activity

Place the 10 prefixes with the stems.

Meter (m)

Prefix	Stem	Full Name	Description	Decimal Description	Equivalent Symbol
giga					
mega					
kilo					
hecto					
deca					
deci					
centi	meter	centimeter	a hundredth of a meter	0.01 m	1 cm
milli					
micro					
nano					

Gram (g)

Prefix	Stem	Full Name	Description	Decimal Description	Equivalent Symbol
giga					
mega					
kilo					
hecto					
deca					
deci					
centi	gram	centigram	a hundredth of a gram	0.01 g	1 cg
milli					
micro					
nano					

Liter (L or l)

Prefix	Stem	Full Name	Description	Decimal Description	Equivalent Symbol
giga					
mega					
kilo					
hecto					
deca					
deci					
centi	liter	centiliter	a hundredth of a liter	0.01 L	1 cL
milli					
micro					
nano					

Name: _____ Date: _____

Symbol Identification Activity

Circle the correct symbol(s) for the prefix and unit listed.

1. decagram   a. DG   b. daG   c. Dg   d. dag

2. megameter   a. mm   b. MM   c. Mm   d. mM

3. nanoliter   a. nl   b. NL   c. nL   d. Nl

4. kilogram   a. Kg   b. kg   c. kG   d. KG

5. decimeter   a. Kg   b. dm   c. DM   d. dM

6. hectoliter   a. HL   b. Hl   c. hl   d. hl

7. micrometer   a. µM   b. µm   c. UM   d. Um

8. gigagram   a. GG   b. Gg   c. gG   d. gg

9. centiliter   a. CL   b. cL   c. cl   d. Cl

10. milligram   a. mG   b. MG   c. mg   d. mg

Extra Credit

dm   mg   nl

Mm   kg   µm

cl   hl   Gg

Prefix Challenge Activity

According to the SI convention on prefix usage, only one prefix may be used at a time. This may pose a problem if you have a thousand billion meters that you want to show in the correct symbol form. If you could use more than one prefix, a thousand billion meters would be:

k (thousand) G (billion) m (meter)

or

kGm

Unfortunately, we cannot do this, so a thousand billion is the same as a trillion. The problem here is that we do not know what the prefix is for a trillion. Listed below is a more complete list of prefixes that include the larger and smaller numbers not listed before.

Prefix Name	Symbol	Decimal Value	Fraction Value	Description
yotta	Y	1,000,000,000,000,000,000,000,000	10^{24}	septillion
zetta	Z	1,000,000,000,000,000,000,000	10^{21}	sextillion
exa	E	1,000,000,000,000,000,000	10^{18}	quintillion
peta	P	1,000,000,000,000,000	10^{15}	quadrillion
tera	T	1,000,000,000,000	10^{12}	trillion
giga	G	1,000,000,000	10^{9}	billion
mega	M	1,000,000	10^{6}	million
kilo	k	1,000	10^{3}	thousand
hecto	h	100	10^{2}	hundred
deca/deka	da	10	10^{1}	ten
deci	d	0.1	1/10 or 10^{-1}	tenth
centi	c	0.01	1/100 or 10^{-2}	hundredth
milli	m	0.00	1/1000 or 10^{-3}	thousandth
micro	μ	0.000 001	10^{-6}	millionth
nano	n	0.000 000 001	10^{-9}	billionth
pico	p	0.000 000 000 001	10^{-12}	trillionth
femto	f	0.000 000 000 000 001	10^{-15}	quadrillionth
atto	a	0.000 000 000 000 000 001	10^{-18}	quintillionth
zepto	z	0.000 000 000 000 000 000 001	10^{-21}	sextillionth
yocto	y	0.000 000 000 000 000 000 000 001	10^{-24}	septillionth

Name:_____ Date:_____

Prefix Challenge Activity (continued)

If a trillion is really a thousand billion, then it is also a million million. Therefore, a trillionth is a thousand billionth and a million millionth. See if you can describe the following numbers in terms of multiples of other numbers.

1. Septillion

_____

_____

_____

_____

2. Quintillionth

_____

_____

_____

_____

3. Sextillion

_____

_____

_____

_____

4. Millionth

_____

_____

_____

_____

Name: _____ Date: _____

Metric Internet Rodeo #2

1. Go to **www.newscientist.com/lastword/answers/lwa78physical.html** and find out what is located 125 yottameters away from Earth.

   _____

2. Stay at the same address and write down what the atomic mass unit can be expressed as in proper SI terms.

   _____

3. Finally at the same address, what is a googol?

   _____

4. Go to **www.planetpets.simplenet.com/plntinsc.htm** and find out how many insects inhabit the earth. How many different species of insects are there?

   _____

5. Go to **forum.swarthmore.edu/dr.math/problems/tondiff.html** and explain what a megagram really is. How does a megagram compare to a short ton or a long ton?

   _____

   _____

6. Go to **forum.swarthmore.edu/dr.math/problems/erba9.17.97.html** and explain what a "flop" is. So what is a terraflop?

   _____

   _____

7. Go to **www.hsu.edu/faculty/worthf/googol.html** and list all of the names of the large numbers and their scientific notations (powers of ten) from septillion to vigintillion.

   _____

   _____

   _____

   _____

   _____

   _____

   _____

Name: _____   Date: _____

Food and Nutrition Activity

The Food and Drug Administration requires all products to be dual labeled with both SI metric and U.S. standard system measurements. However, it is likely that many manufacturers have placed the incorrect symbols on the net quantity of contents statement. An example of the net quantity of contents statement is:

Net Wt. 10 3/4 oz. (305 g)

Divide the class into 6 equal groups. Assign each group one of the following Food Group Pyramid groups:
1. Fats, oils, and sweets
2. Milk, yogurt, and cheese
3. Meat, poultry, fish, dry beans, eggs, nuts
4. Vegetables
5. Fruits
6. Bread, cereal, rice, pasta

Have each student in each group bring in two net quantity of contents statements from products within his/her group. Then fill out the table below. You may need to make extra copies of the table.

Food Group: _____

Product Name	Brand Name	Net Quantity of Contents Statement

Name: _____ Date: _____

After all groups have completely filled out their information, find out if any had incorrect statements on their products. If so:
1. Find the address of the company that makes that product.
2. Write a tactful letter to the President/CEO of the company explaining your class' project and their findings.
3. In the letter, ask that the product's net quantity of contents statement be changed in the near future to present the correct SI metric unit symbols.
4. If your class receives a response, write a return letter thanking the company for its prompt consideration of the problem.

If your class was not able to find any errors, pick out several products and write letters to compliment the company on their excellent use of the SI metric symbols.

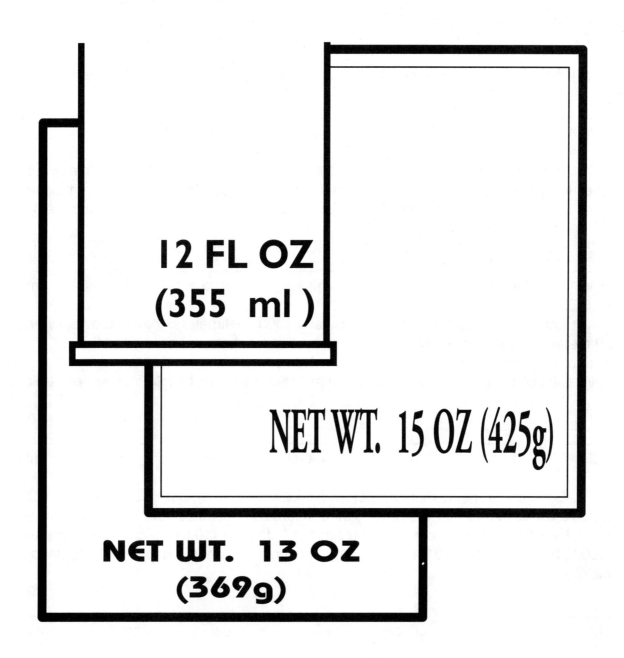

Metric Measurements

To better understand the metric system of measurement, you must actually measure using metric devices. Acquire the metric measuring devices to measure length (meters), volume (liters), and weight (grams or kilograms.) If these devices have both the SI and U.S. standards on them, cover up the U.S. standard measures so that only the SI metric may be used.

Students need to be able to convert centimeters to meters, millimeters to centimeters, and vice versa for length, volume, and weight. To do so, the students can use a familiar tool - the place value diagram as seen below.

Thousands	Hundreds	Tens	Units	Tenths	Hundredths	Thousandths
___	___	___	___	___	___	___

If the place value diagram is modified, it can easily show the metric prefixes as follows:

___	___	___	___	___	___	___
kilo	hecto	deca	units	deci	centi	milli

From the place value diagram, the student knows that the hundreds place is ten times larger than the tens place, a hundred times larger than the units place, a thousand times larger than the tenths place, etc. The same relationship exists with metric prefixes.

0	0	1	0	0	0	0
kilo	hecto	deca	meter	deci	centi	milli

Look at the diagram above. If you have 1000 centimeters, then you actually have 10 meters or one decameter. You know this because the number is 10 to the left of the word meter and the number 1 resides in the deca space of the metric prefix diagram. If you have 100,000 centimeters, you actually have 1,000 meters or 1 kilolmeter, as seen below.

1	0	0	0	0	0	0
kilo	hecto	deca	meter	deci	centi	milli

Look at the metric diagram below. Notice that the number 1 is to the right of the word liter. This means that you have to think in terms of decimals now. In this example you have 1 centiliter. This means that you have 0.1 deciliters, 0.01 liters, 0.001 decaliters, 0.0001 hectoliters, 0.00001 kiloliters, etc. Of course you should notice that you have 10 milliliters.

0	0	0	0	0	1	0
kilo	hecto	deca	liter	deci	centi	milli

Name: _____ Date: _____

Metric Place Value Activity #1

Look at the metric diagrams below and answer the following questions.

0	0	0	0	0	0	1
___	___	___	gram	___	___	___

0	1	0	0	0	0	0
___	___	___	meter	___	___	___

1. How many grams and meters do you have?

_____

2. How many milligrams and millimeters do you have?

_____

3. How many hectograms and hectometers do you have?

_____

4. How many decigrams and decimeters do you have?

_____

5. How many kilograms and kilometers do you have?

_____

6. How many centigrams and centimeters do you have?

_____

$$25\ g = 250\ dg = 2500\ cg = 25000\ mg$$

Name:_____ Date:_____

Metric Place Value Activity #2

Look at the metric diagrams below and answer the following questions.

1	2	5	0	0	0	0
___	___	___	___ liter	___	___	___

0	0	0	3	9	8	5
___	___	___	___ gram	___	___	___

1. How many kiloliters do you have?

_____

2. How many decaliters do you have?

_____

3. How many milliliters do you have?

_____

4. How many centigrams do you have?

_____

5. How many kilograms do you have?

_____

6. How many decigrams do you have?

_____

0.001 km = 1 m = 100 cm = 1000 m

Name: _____ Date: _____

Measurement Activity

Get three tables and bring them into your classroom. Select the following items and place on the first table, which will be designated for measuring length:

• piece of chalk, eraser, book, 3.5 inch floppy disk, computer case, frisbee.

Select the following items and place on the second table, which will be designated for measuring volume:

• six different flasks or containers with different levels of colored water in each.

Select the following items and place them on the third table, which will be designated for measuring mass:

• eraser, book, bag of beans or rice, a basketball, a baseball, and a medium-sized balloon (do not attempt to air the balloon up).

On each table you need to place enough measuring devices to allow several students to work at one time. Divide the class into three groups. Have each group guess the measurement of each item on all three tables and put their guesses in the charts provided below and on the next page. Then have the students actually measure each item on all three tables using only the devices you provide. The students need to record the measurements in the charts, as well.

Chart 1: Length

Item	Guess Measurement	Actual Measurement
Piece of chalk	_____	_____
Eraser	_____	_____
Book	_____	_____
3.5 inch floppy diskette	_____	_____
Computer case	_____	_____
Frisbee	_____	_____

Chart 2: Volume

Item	Guess Measurement	Actual Measurement
Flask #1	_____	_____
Flask #2	_____	_____
Flask #3	_____	_____
Flask #4	_____	_____
Flask #5	_____	_____
Flask #6	_____	_____

Name: _____ Date: _____

Table 3: Weight

Item	Guess Measurement	Actual Measurement
Eraser	_____	_____
Book	_____	_____
Bag of beans or rice	_____	_____
Basketball	_____	_____
Baseball	_____	_____
Medium-sized balloon	_____	_____

Now, convert all actual measurements to kilo, hecto, deca, units, deci, centi, and milli metric measurements, for the piece of chalk, flask #3, and the baseball.

Chalk	Flask #3	Baseball
kilometer	kiloliter	kilogram
_____	_____	_____
hectometer	hectoliter	hectogram
_____	_____	_____
decameter	decaliter	decagram
_____	_____	_____
meter	liter	gram
_____	_____	_____
decimeter	deciliter	decigram
_____	_____	_____
centimeter	centiliter	centigram
_____	_____	_____
millimeter	milliliter	milligram
_____	_____	_____

Name: _____ Date: _____

Body Ruler Activity

    People often associate length and weight with parts of their bodies. In this activity, measure the following parts of your body and record the measurements below. Then use these measurements to estimate the length of the teacher's desk, the width of the chalk board, the length of the room, height of the bottom of the chalkboard from the floor, and the distance around the gymnasium.

    Width of handspan from thumb to little finger when completely spread _____

    Width of index finger on right hand _____

    Height from floor to top of head _____

    Length of both arms extended horizontally _____

    Length of one step from heel of right foot to toe of left foot _____

Teacher's desk is _____ .

Width of the chalkboard is _____ .

Length of the room is _____ .

Distance from floor to the bottom of the chalkboard is _____ .

Distance around the gymnasium is _____ .

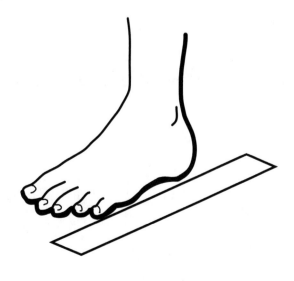

Name: _____ Date: _____

Reasonable Measurement Activity

Choose the most reasonable measurement.

1. Thickness of a dime   a. 1 m   b. 1 cm   c. 1 mm

2. Glass of water   a. 250 kL   b. 250 mL   c. 250 L

3. Weight of a pencil   a. 10 mg   b. 10 g   c. 10 kg

4. Full tank of gas   a. 30 L   b. 30 kL   c. 30 mL

Complete the following.

5. 25 g = _____ kg   11. 803 mL = _____ kL

6. 89.7 L = _____ mL   12. 4 mg = _____ hg

7. 125 mm = _____ km   13. 850 dm = _____ dam

8. 2350 kg = _____ mg   14. 0.11 L = _____ daL

9. 0.001 hm = _____ m   15. 2235 kg = _____ g

10. 0.975 g = _____ mg   16. 10.5 mL = _____ L

Circle the correct answer.

17. Which is larger?   a. 25 mL   b. 25 hL   c. 25 dL   d. 25 daL

18. Which is longer?   a. 135 m   b. 135 hm   c. 135 dm   d. 135 mm

19. Which is heavier?   a. 0.1 mg   b. 0.1 g   c. 0.1 kg   d. 0.1 cg

Metrics in Science

Science is the predominant reason that the metric system came into being. French scientists needed to standardize their results so these results would be fully understood by the rest of the scientific community. As a result, many different SI units were developed.

Ampere - basic unit of electric current
Kelvin - basic unit of temperature for scientific purposes
Mole - basic unit of substance
Candela - basic unit of luminous intensity
Farad - capacity to store elecricity
Hertz - one cycle per second
Joule - basic unit of work or energy
Newton - basic unit of force
Ohm - unit of resistance of an electrical conductor
Pascal - basic unit of pressure
Volt - unit of electrical potential
Watt - used to measure the power or the rate of doing work

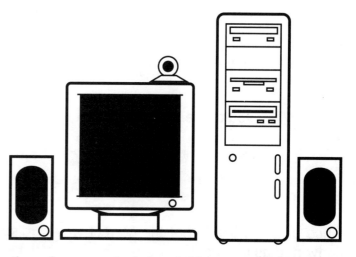

The most common unit is **hertz** (Hz). We see this used constantly in descriptions of computer components. For example, the computer has a 400 megahertz processor. What this really means is that the processor can execute up to 400 million basic operations per second. The computer video card has a 60 Hz refresh rate. This simply means that the video card sends 60 signals per second to the monitor, which allows for the monitor to appear without waves or lines. While not listed as a standard unit of SI, the notion of a computer's hard drive or random access memory (RAM) is also metric. A computer that has a 6 gigabyte hard drive and 64 megabytes of RAM is capable of storing 64 million bytes of computer information and can keep up to 64 million bytes of computer programming in use at any given second.

Volt is another common term. We see that most appliances need 110 volts or 220 volts of electricity to operate. **Amps** are commonly used in fuses and circuit breakers. A 15-amp circuit breaker trips or activates when too much current is drawn by the circuit. This keeps our appliances from overloading with current and catching fire.

Scientific Numbers

Science is wonderful, but it has a tendency to deal with very large and very small numbers, and it must therefore deal with what is known as scientific numbers or notation. **Scientific notation** is simply a number from 1 to 9 in the units (ones) place and as many numbers to the right of the decimal place as needed times 10 to a power. For example, the earth's mass is:

$$5.98 \times 10^{24} \text{ kg.}$$

Notice that the number 5 is in the units (ones) place with 9 and 8 to the right of the decimal place. You can see that this number is multiplying the number 10 to the 24th power.

When you multiply two scientific numbers, you do the following:

$$5.98 \times 10^{24} \quad X \quad 2.35 \times 10^{5} \quad = \quad 5.98 \times 2.35 \text{ and } 10^{24} \quad x \quad 10^{5}$$

$$= \quad 14.053 \times 10^{24+5} \quad = \quad 14.053 \times 10^{29}.$$

However, 14.053 is not the correct way to show a scientific number. $14.053 = 1.4053 \times 10^{1}$.

Now combine the two powers of 10 as follows: $10^{1} \times 10^{29} = 10^{30}$. So the final answer to the problem is 1.4053×10^{30}.

When you divide two scientific numbers, you do the following:

$$5.6 \times 10^{15} \quad \div \quad 8.3 \times 10^{5} \quad = \quad 5.6 \div 8.3 \quad x \quad 10^{15} \div 10^{5}$$

$$= \quad 0.675 \times 10^{15-5} \quad = \quad 0.675 \times 10^{10}.$$

Once again, 0.675 is not the correct way to display a scientific number, so it must be converted as follows:

$$0.675 \quad = \quad 6.75 \times 10^{-1}$$

Now, 0.675×10^{10} becomes $6.75 \times 10^{-1} \times 10^{10} = 6.75^{-1+10} = 6.75 \times 10^{9}$.

Name: _____ Date: _____

Scientific Number Activity

Find the product or quotient of the following scientific numbers:

1. 2.35×10^5 X 1.25×10^{13} _____

2. 9.9×10^{21} X 5.5×10^{17} _____

3. 6.75×10^{11} X 8.55×10^2 _____

4. 1.11×10^8 X 1.5×10^2 _____

5. 2.995×10^{20} ÷ 3.668×10^{12} _____

6. 7.75×10^{12} ÷ 2.33×10^7 _____

7. 8.4×10^{20} ÷ 4.2×10^{10} _____

8. 9.75×10^{19} X 2.32×10^{12} ÷ 4.51×10^{22} _____

Name: _____ Date: _____

Scientific Number Challenge Activity

The escape velocity for a rocket to leave the gravitational force of a planet is the formula:

$$v = \frac{2GM}{r}$$

Where **v** = the minimum velocity required, **G** is the gravitational constant 6.67×10^{-11}, **M** is the mass of the planet in kilograms, and **r** is the radius of the planet in meters.

Compute the escape velocity for the indicated planet using the formula above.

1. Uranus: Mass is 8.73×10^{25} kg, radius is 2.35×10^7 m. _____

2. Venus: Mass is 4.0×10^{24} kg, radius is 6.06×10^6 m. _____

3. Jupiter: Mass is 1.90×10^{27} kg, radius is 7.15×10^7 m. _____

4. Earth: Mass is 5.98×10^{24} kg, radius is 6.37×10^6 m. _____

Name: _____   Date: _____

Electricity Activity

As a class, write a letter to a local electrician explaining that you are currently studying the metric system. You would like him or her to come to your classroom and provide a basic explanation of the terms **volts** and **amps**. Ask the electrician to explain how the circuit box works and how the circuit breakers function in a house.

After the explanation of how a circuit breaker works, bring in several appliances and check their ratings to see if you could plug all of them into a circuit running on a 15-amp breaker. The rule of thumb is to take the amperage (in this case 15) and subtract 20 percent to determine the safety code requirement. Then take the safety code requirement and multiply the voltage of the system (in this case 120). The maximum watts allowed on a 15-amp circuit on a 120-volt line is 1440 watts.

Bring in a toaster, a coffee pot, a small television, a fan, and a blender. Look on these items to find the number of watts each appliance requires and fill in the table below.

Appliance	Wattage Needed
Toaster	
Coffee Pot	
Small Television	
Fan	
Blender	
Total Wattage	

1. Can your 15-amp circuit handle all of the appliances at one time?

_____

2. Which appliances can you plug in at the same time? Provide at least three **different** options.

_____

_____

_____

3. In order to allow all of your appliances to work at the same time, what size amp breaker is needed?

_____

Name: _____   Date: _____

Wattage Activity

There are two kinds of circuit breakers that are used in circuit boxes: single-pole and double-pole. The single-pole breaker is used for 120-volt circuits that require only one "hot" wire. The double-pole breaker is used for 240-volt circuits, such as your clothes dryer, electric cook stove, furnace, and central air system, all of which require two "hot" wires.

To figure the wattage for each type of breaker, you must use the safety code requirement of subtracting 20 percent of the amperage first. Then multiply by the number of volts on the circuit. For a 20-amp double-pole breaker, do not double the 20 amps to 40 amps. The breaker is still only a 20-amp breaker.

Find the number of watts allowed according to safety code requirements for the following.

1. A 60-amp double-pole breaker on a 240-volt circuit. _____

2. A 30-amp breaker on a 120-volt circuit. _____

3. A 40-amp breaker on a 120-volt circuit. _____

4. A 40-amp double-pole breaker on a 240-volt circuit._____

5. A 20-amp double-pole breaker on a 240-volt circuit._____

6. A 30-amp double-pole breaker on a 240-volt circuit. _____

Name: _____ Date: _____

Metric Internet Rodeo #3

1. Go to **http://inf.er.usgs.gov/fact-sheets/finding-your-way/description.html** and write down what one centimeter represents on the following map scales:

   a. 1:20,000 _____

   b. 1:62,500 _____

   c. 1:50,000 _____

   d. 1:250,000 _____

   e. 1:1,000,000 _____

2. Go to **http://www.sciencemadesimple.com/~science/Conversion.html** and convert the following:

   a. Area: 64 square feet to square centimeters _____

   b. Length: 50,000 inches to kilometers _____

   c. Temperature: 0°F to degrees Celsius _____

      212°F to degrees Celsius _____

      30°C to degrees Fahrenheit _____

      -10°C to degrees Fahrenheit _____

   d. Volume: 25 liters to cubic centimeters _____

   e. Weight: 25 pounds to milligrams _____

3. Go to **http://www.exploratorium.edu/ronh/solar_system** and find the scaled measures for the following if the Sun had a diameter of 254 mm:

   a. the radius of the orbit of the earth around the Sun in meters _____

   b. the diameter of Uranus in millimeters _____

   c. the distance to Sirius in kilometers _____

   d. the size of a white dwarf in millimeters _____

Metrics in Business Applications

The "Almighty Dollar," the French franc, the German deutsche mark, the Japanese yen, and the British pound are reasons why the world has gone metric. The economy of any one country has become increasingly dependent on the economies of other countries. The United States has seen this become more predominant since the end of World War II. In 1945 the United Sates owned up to 40 percent of the gross world product. In 1970 this percentage had slipped to only about 15 percent of the gross world product. In 1995 the United States owned only about 10 percent of the gross world product.

Why the slip? One reason is metrics. The world had gone metric, and the United States failed to keep up with the labeling of export products. Other nations refused to buy products that were not made to their metric standards. After all, it is much more expensive to maintain two sets of tools—metric and U.S. standard. This expense is well known to auto mechanics here in the United States.

So exactly who uses the metric system in America? Medicine manufacturers, the scientific community, the food industry, the liquor industry, the automotive industry, the U.S. Armed Forces, and of course, all U.S. governmental agencies.

Consider the problem of exportation and importation. The United States utilizes the standard ton, which weighs 2000 pounds. However, the metric ton is 1000 kilograms, which is 2205 pounds. U.S. business must account for the differences in weights in order to price the product for other countries. This process can potentially be profitable or detrimental, depending on the other countries' willingness to pay our price, or even the United States' willingness to pay the price for an imported product.

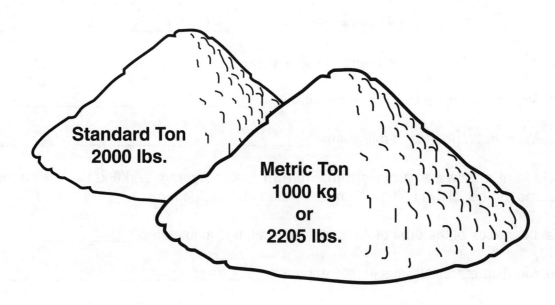

Standard Ton
2000 lbs.

Metric Ton
1000 kg
or
2205 lbs.

Name: _____ Date: _____

Tool Activity

Auto mechanics use two sets of tools to work on most American and foreign automobiles. This is necessary because so many vehicles were produced prior to the major conversion to the metric system of the U.S. automakers.

Convert the following fractions to decimals (round to the thousandths place.)

1. 1/8 _____	13. 1/2 _____
2. 5/32 _____	14. 17/32 _____
3. 3/16 _____	15. 9/16 _____
4. 7/32 _____	16. 19/32 _____
5. 1/4 _____	17. 5/8 _____
6. 9/32 _____	18. 21/32 _____
7. 5/16 _____	19. 11/16 _____
8. 11/32 _____	20. 23/32 _____
9. 3/8 _____	21. 3/4 _____
10. 13/32 _____	22. 25/32 _____
11. 7/16 _____	23. 13/16 _____
12. 15/32 _____	24. 27/32 _____

Now convert the following metric sizes into decimal inches and round to the nearest thousandths (1 mm equals 0.03937 inches):

1. 1 mm _____	13. 13 mm _____
2. 2 mm _____	14. 14 mm _____
3. 3 mm _____	15. 15 mm _____
4. 4 mm _____	16. 16 mm _____
5. 5 mm _____	17. 17 mm _____
6. 6 mm _____	18. 18 mm _____
7. 7 mm _____	19. 19 mm _____
8. 8 mm _____	20. 20 mm _____
9. 9 mm _____	21. 21 mm _____
10. 10 mm _____	22. 22 mm _____
11. 11 mm _____	23. 23 mm _____
12. 12 mm _____	24. 24 mm _____

Name:_____ Date: _____

Now place the fraction and millimeter sizes in order from least to greatest according to their decimal equivalents.

1. _____

2. _____

3. _____

4. _____

5. _____

6. _____

7. _____

8. _____

9. _____

10. _____

11. _____

12. _____

13. _____

14. _____

15. _____

16. _____

17. _____

18. _____

19. _____

20. _____

21. _____

22. _____

23. _____

24. _____

25. _____

26. _____

27. _____

28. _____

29. _____

30. _____

31. _____

32. _____

33. _____

34. _____

35. _____

36. _____

37. _____

38. _____

39. _____

40. _____

41. _____

42. _____

43. _____

44. _____

45. _____

46. _____

47. _____

48. _____

Name: _____   Date: _____

Tonnage Conversion Activity

In 1997 China imported 13,230,000 metric tons of steel.

1. If the United States exported 40 percent of this amount of steel, how many metric tons would this be?

   _____

2. If the cost per metric ton was $15.00, how much money did the United States take in for the steel?

   _____

3. Now convert the number of metric tons to U.S. standard tons (1 metric ton equals 2205 pounds and the U.S. standard ton equals 2000 pounds.)

   _____

4. Assume that the United States paid $12.50 per standard ton for the steel, how much did the company pay in total for the exported steel?

   _____

5. Did the U.S. company make a profit? (Profit equals revenue minus cost.) If so, how much?

   _____

6. Can a U.S. company sell the product in metric tons for the same amount it pays for it in standard tons and still make a profit? Why or why not?

   _____

   _____

7. Can a U.S. company pay for an imported product and charge the same amount in the United States and make a profit? Why or why not?

   _____

   _____

37

Comparison of U.S. Standard to Metric Standard

The greatest problem for most students lies in conversions from U.S. standard measures to metric and vice versa. The following tables are provided as a tool for speeding the conversion process.

Length

	cm	m	km	in.	ft.	yd.	mi.
1cm	1	0.01	0.00001	0.3937	0.03281	0.01094	0.000006214
1m	100	1	0.001	39.37	3.281	1.094	0.0006214
1km	100000	1000	1	39370	3281	1094	0.6214
1 in.	2.54	0.0254	0.0000254	1	0.0833	0.0278	0.00001578
1 ft.	30.48	0.3048	0.003048	12	1	0.3333	0.0001894
1 yd.	91.44	0.9144	0.0009144	36	3	1	0.0005682
1 mi.	160930	1609.3	1.6093	63360	5280	1760	1

Area

	cm^2	m^2	in.^{2}	ft.^{2}	acre	mi.^{2}
1 cm^2	1	0.0001	0.1550	0.001076	0.0000000247	0.00000000003861
1 m^2	10000	1	1550	10.76	0.0002471	0.0000003861
1 in.^{2}	6.452	0.0006452	1	0.006944	0.0000001594	0.0000000002491
1 ft.^{2}	929	0.0929	144	1	0.00002296	0.00000003587
1 acre	40470000	4407	6273000	43560	1	0.001563
1 mi.^{2}	25900000000	2590000	4007000000	27880000	640	1

Volume

	cm^3	m^3	in.^{3}	ft.^{3}	L	oz.	gal.
1 cm^3	1	0.000001	0.06102	0.00003531	0.001	0.03381	0.0002642
1 m^3	1000000	1	61020	35.31	1000	33810	264.2
1 in.^{3}	16.39	0.00001639	1	0.0005787	0.01639	0.5541	0.004329
1 ft.^{3}	28320	0.02832	1728	1	28.32	957.5	7.480
1 L	1000	0.001	61.03	0.03532	1	33.81	0.2642
1 oz.	29.57	0.00002957	1.805	0.001044	0.02957	1	0.007813
1 gal.	3785	0.003785	231	0.1337	3.785	128	1

Weight

	g	kg	oz.	lb.	U.S. ton
1 g	1	0.001	0.03527	0.002205	0.000001102
1 kg	1000	1	35.27	2.205	0.001102
1 oz.	28.35	0.02835	1	0.0625	0.00003125
1 lb..	453.6	0.4536	16	1	0.0005
1 U.S. ton	907200	907.2	32000	2000	1

38

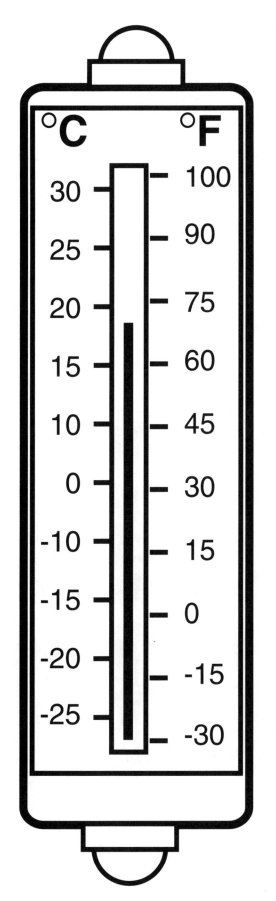

Temperature

To convert from °F to °C use this formula:

$$°C = 5/9 \times (°F - 32)$$

To convert from °C to °F use this formula:

$$°F = 9/5 \times °C + 32$$

Here is a rhyme to help remember general metric temperatures:

Thirty is hot
Twenty is nice
Ten is chilly
Zero is ice.

Name: _____ Date: _____

Track and Field Activity

High schools and junior high schools frequently participate in track and field events consisting of running, jumping, throwing, and leaping. All events began using the U.S. standards of 110 yds., 220 yds., 330 yds., 440 yds., 880 yds., and 1760 yds. for all running events.

Here are some common track and field distances. You must convert from metric to the equivalent U.S. standard and vice versa. (For all running events, round all meter distances to the nearest hundred and all yard distances to one of the measures listed above.)

1. 100-meter dash = _____ yard dash

2. 880-yard run = _____ meter run

3. 1600-meter relay = _____ yard relay

4. A shot put record throw of 40 feet 7 inches = _____ centimeters

5. A discus toss of 55.5 meters = _____ inches

6. 330-yard hurdles = _____ meter hurdles

7. A pole vault attempt of 12 feet 6 inches = _____ centimeters

8. A shot put weighing 4 kg = _____ pounds

9. A long-jump record of 15 feet 1 inch = _____ meters

10. A 1760-yard run = _____ meter run

40

Name: _____   Date: _____

Conversion Comparison Activity

Another great reason for using metrics is the ease of computation. Consider the following problem:

1'5" x 2'4" = [1' + (5/12) x [2' + (4/12)] = 1.4167 x 2.3333 = 3.3056 square feet

or the metric equivalent

0.4318 m x 0.7112 m = 0.3071 m²

Which seemed easier to you?

Now try these U.S. standard and metric problems (these are not equivalent problems).

1. 1 yd. x 3'8" - (2'2" x 1'3") _____   2. 5'4" x 3 yd. _____

3. 6.5 m x 4.2 m - (0.25 m x 3.1 m) _____   4. 250 mm x 47.5 cm _____

5. 4 mi. - 2500' + 2900" _____   6. 5 mi. x (5'3" + 2'6") _____

7. 25 m - 650 cm + 2320 mm _____   8. 8 km x (4 m + 34 mm) _____

Name: _____   Date: _____

Internet Conversion Calculator Activity

Go to **http://www.sciencemadesimple.com/~science/Conversion.html** and convert the following:

Area

	cm²	m²	in.²	ft.²	acre	mi.²
12 cm²						
1.5 m²						
125 in.²						
31.25 ft.²						
2.5 acre						
0.575 mi.²						

Length

	cm	m	km	in.	ft.	yd.	mi.
239 cm							
1525 m							
16.95 km							
24675 in.							
0.35 ft.							
8.75 yd.							
23.5 mi.							

Volume

	cm³	m³	in.³	ft.³	L	oz.	gal.
0.25 cm³							
15.7 m³							
318 in.³							
35.25 ft.³							
10 L							
24 oz.							
55 gal.							

Name: _____ Date: _____

Weight

	g	kg	oz.	lb.	U.S. ton
15535 g					
115.55 kg					
246.75 oz.					
28955.6 lb.					
12.25 U.S. ton					

Fruit

Convert 250 apples into oranges. _____

Convert the following:

1. 25000 mL into cm^3 _____

2. 5 km^2 into acres _____

3. 250 in.^{3} into milliliters _____

4. 120°C into °F _____

5. 98°F into °C _____

Name: _____   Date: _____

Length Conversion Activity

Use this table to compute the problems below.

	cm	m	km	in.	ft.	yd.	mi.
1cm	1	0.01	0.00001	0.3937	0.03281	0.01094	0.000006214
1m	100	1	0.001	39.37	3.281	1.094	0.0006214
1km	100000	1000	1	39370	3281	1094	0.6214
1 in.	2.54	0.0254	0.0000254	1	0.0833	0.0278	0.00001578
1 ft.	30.48	0.3048	0.003048	12	1	0.3333	0.0001894
1 yd.	91.44	0.9144	0.0009144	36	3	1	0.0005682
1 mi.	160930	1609.3	1.6093	63360	5280	1760	1

Convert the following into inches.

1. 33 cm

2. 284 ft.

3. 64 mi.

4. 24.22 km

_____   _____   _____   _____

5. 87 ft. 5.5 in.

6. 12 yd. 4 ft. 4 in.

7. 9 mi. 52 yd.

8. 0.0025 m

_____   _____   _____   _____

Convert the following to meters.

9. 8.9 ft.

10. 2 mi.

11. 29,000 cm

12. 12.57 yd.

_____   _____   _____   _____

13. 95.756 km

14. 5 mi. 100 yd.

15. 255 ft. 7.5 in.

16. 25 yd. 2 ft. 5 in.

_____   _____   _____   _____

Name: _____ Date: _____

Area Conversion Activity

Use this table to compute the problems below.

	cm²	m²	in²	ft²	acre	mi²
1 cm²	1	0.0001	0.1550	0.001076	0.0000000247	0.00000000003861
1 m²	10000	1	1550	10.76	0.0002471	0.0000003861
1 in²	6.452	0.0006452	1	0.006944	0.0000001594	0.0000000002491
1 ft²	929	0.0929	144	1	0.00002296	0.00000003587
1 acre	40470000	4407	6273000	43560	1	0.001563
1 mi²	25900000000	2590000	4007000000	27880000	640	1

Convert the following to square miles.

1. 29,000 acres

2. 7556 in.²

3. 92.5 m²

4. 957,100 cm²

_____   _____   _____   _____

5. 274 ft.²

6. 0.125 cm²

7. 0.975 m²

8. 7 acres and 500 ft.²

_____   _____   _____   _____

Convert the following to square centimeters.

9. 81 mi.²

10. 920 ft.²

11. 294.5 m²

12. 800 in.²

_____   _____   _____   _____

13. 22.5 acres

14. 0.756 m²

15. 0.215 mi.²

16. 0.0222 in.²

_____   _____   _____   _____

Name: _____   Date: _____

Volume Conversion Activity

Use this table to compute the problems below.

	cm³	m³	in.³	ft.³	L	oz.	gal.
1 cm³	1	0.000001	0.06102	0.00003531	0.001	0.03381	0.0002642
1 m³	1000000	1	61020	35.31	1000	33810	264.2
1 in.³	16.39	0.00001639	1	0.0005787	0.01639	0.5541	0.004329
1 ft.³	28320	0.02832	1728	1	28.32	957.5	7.480
1 L	1000	0.001	61.03	0.03532	1	33.81	0.2642
1 oz.	29.57	0.00002957	1.805	0.001044	0.02957	1	0.007813
1 gal.	3785	0.003785	231	0.1337	3.785	128	1

Convert the following to liters.

1. 350 in.³

2. 550 gal.

3. 9500 cm³

4. 35.55 ft.³

_____   _____   _____   _____

5. 75555 oz.

6. 97.75 m³

7. 0.0125 gal.

8. 0.55 ft.³

_____   _____   _____   _____

Convert the following into cubic inches.

9. 77.5 L

10. 375 cm³

11. 74.25 ft.³

12. 85.4 gal.

_____   _____   _____   _____

13. 9250 oz.

14. 29.75 m³

15. 0.057 ft.³

16. 0.255 L

_____   _____   _____   _____

Name: _____ Date: _____

Weight Conversion Activity

Use this table to compute the problems below.

	g	kg	oz.	lb.	U.S. ton
1 g	1	0.001	0.03527	0.002205	0.000001102
1 kg	1000	1	35.27	2.205	0.001102
1 oz.	28.35	0.02835	1	0.0625	0.00003125
1 lb.	453.6	0.4536	16	1	0.0005
1 U.S. ton	907200	907.2	32000	2000	1

Convert the following to kilograms.

1. 25,550 g

2. 5.975 ton

3. 875.4 lb.

4. 1234 oz.

_____   _____   _____   _____

5. 0.024 ton

6. 8.75 g

7. 0.255 lb.

8. 0.15 oz.

_____   _____   _____   _____

Convert the following to pounds.

9. 88.975 kg

10. 255.6 ton

11. 87,775 g

12. 91.5 oz.

_____   _____   _____   _____

13. 0.22 ton

14. 7.25 g

15. 0.75 kg

16. 85,000 oz.

_____   _____   _____   _____

47

Name: _____ Date: _____

Temperature Conversion Activity

Use the formula below to convert from Celsius to Fahrenheit.

°F = 9/5 x °C + 32

1. 29°C   2. 85°C   3. -10°C   4. 17°C

_____   _____   _____   _____

5. -100°C   6. 145°C   7. 1°C   8. 30°C

_____   _____   _____   _____

Use the formula below to convert from Fahrenheit to Celsius.

°C = 5/9 x (°F - 32)

9. 29°F   10. 85°F   11. -10°F   12. 17°F

_____   _____   _____   _____

13. -100°F   14. 145°F   15. 1°F   16. 30°F

_____   _____   _____   _____

Use a dual-scale thermometer or the formulas above to convert the following problems.

17. 25 °F   _____   22. 25°C   _____

18. 30°C   _____   23. 30°F   _____

19. 0°F   _____   24. 0°C   _____

20. 100°C   _____   25. 100°F   _____

21. 150°F   _____   26. 150°C   _____

48

Name: _____ Date: _____

Conversion Practice Activity

Convert the following to centimeters.

1. 78.5 in.   2. 193.7 hm   3. 0.88 mi.   4. 0.002 ft.

_____   _____   _____   _____

Convert the following to square inches.

5. 0.911 cm²   6. 81490 ft.²   7. 0.2121 mi.²   8. 0.2359 acres

_____   _____   _____   _____

Convert the following to cubic centimeters.

9. 2.55 L   10. 12.1 gal.   11. 0.0025 ft.³   12. 0.095 m³

_____   _____   _____   _____

Convert the following to grams.

13. 103.75 lb.   14. 0.2075 U.S.ton   15. 8673 oz.   16. 19.765 kg

_____   _____   _____   _____

Convert the following to Celsius.

17. 27.5°F   18. 153°F   19. -22°F   20. 2.5°F

_____   _____   _____   _____

Convert the following to Fahrenheit.

21. 27.5°C   22. 153°C   23. -22°C   24. 2.5°C

_____   _____   _____   _____

49

Name: _____ Date: _____

Solar System Activity

Let's build our solar system on a toilet paper roll. That is correct, a toilet paper roll. If you go to **http://www.exploratorium.edu/ronh/solar_system**, you will see an activity on building a solar system. What is wonderful about this activity is that it provides the ability to compute planet sizes and radii from the Sun in both U.S. standard and metric. It also provides the actual metric sizes and radii for each planet as well.

In the green box at the website, place the number "10." Now click on "calculate" and watch out. The program executes, and you can now print out the results.

What this printout tells you is that if the Sun were 10 mm in diameter, each planet would be a specified size accordingly and its radius from the Sun would also be scaled accordingly. Now draw a 10 mm size dot on the first sheet of toilet paper.

Next, start rolling out the toilet paper and then draw Mercury 416 mm away from the Sun. Continue drawing all nine planets on the toilet paper the distance according to the scaled radius in meters (convert to millimeters if more convenient.)

After all nine planets have been completed, take the roll of toilet paper outside or in the gymnasium and unroll it completely. Have the students stand at the spots that correspond with each planet. Now they will get a good understanding of how vast space really is.

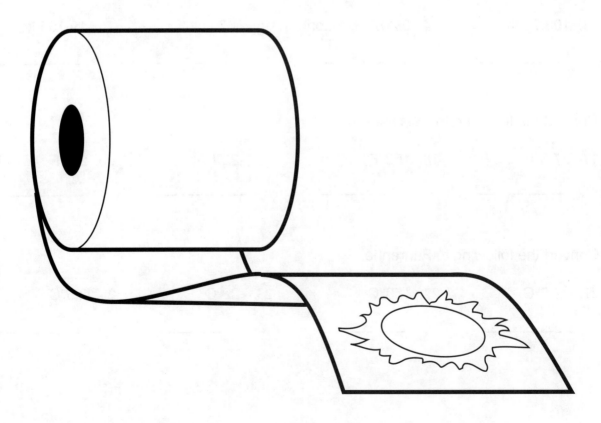

Name: _____ Date: _____

Let's Make Cookies Activity

The old saying, "The way to a man's heart is through his stomach," is also true for education. The way to get a student's attention is to offer food.

Each student needs to bring in his or her favorite cookie recipe from home. Remind the students that pre-made cookie dough does not constitute a recipe. Have each student present his or her recipe and explain why it is his or her favorite. After all students have presented their recipes, take a vote as to which one you will make as a class.

Once it has been chosen, copy the recipe for each student. Then have each student convert the U.S. standard measures to metric. **Be aware**—there are two different ounce measures, one dry and one liquid. Now have each student convert the recipe to metric measures.

Group the students together and assign them an ingredient to bring in the next day. Now the fun begins. After all the ingredients are brought in, use only metric devices and make the cookie dough. If you have dual-scale devices, make sure you cover up the U.S. standard measures so that only metric measures can be used.

Bake the cookies and watch the smiles grow. There is little doubt that the students will not fail to pay attention on this activity.

Use the following weight and volume conversions.

Volume/Weight	Metric Unit
1 teaspoon	4.929 mL
1 tablespoon	14.79 mL
1 fluid ounce	29.57 mL
1 cup	236.6 mL
1 pint	473.2 mL
1 quart	946.3 mL
1 gallon	3.785 L
1 dry ounce	28.25 g

Name: _____ Date: _____

Combination Metric Conversions Activity #1

Unfortunately, not all problems involve only one conversion. Sometimes it is necessary to do two, three, or more conversions before the problem is completed.

For example, convert 20 miles per hour to meters per second. The best way to do the conversion is to handle one unit at a time. First, rewrite the problem as a fraction. ("Per" means division.)

$$\frac{20 \text{ miles}}{\text{hour}}$$

Since you are converting from miles to meters, you then write the conversion factor as a fraction as well.

$$\frac{1609.3 \text{ meters}}{1 \text{ mile}}$$

Keep in mind that if "miles" was the numerator in the first fraction, it will be the denominator in the conversion and vice versa.

Now multiply both fractions together.

$$\frac{20 \text{ miles}}{\text{hour}} \quad X \quad \frac{1609.3 \text{ meters}}{1 \text{ mile}} \quad = \quad \frac{32186 \text{ meters}}{\text{hour}}$$

It is time to convert the hour to seconds. Write the conversion fraction with the hour as the numerator and seconds as the denominator and then multiply.

$$\frac{1 \text{ hour}}{3600 \text{ seconds}}$$

$$\frac{32186 \text{ meters}}{\text{hour}} \quad X \quad \frac{1 \text{ hour}}{3600 \text{ seconds}} \quad = \quad \frac{32186 \text{ meters}}{3600 \text{ seconds}}$$

Finally, divide the 32186 by 3600. The answer is 8.941 meters per second.

Name: _____ Date: _____

Convert the following problems using the method above.

1. 800 meters per second to miles per hour

$$\frac{800 \text{ m}}{\text{sec.}} \quad X \quad \frac{1 \text{ mi.}}{1609.2 \text{ m}} \quad X \quad \frac{3600 \text{ sec.}}{1 \text{ hr.}} \quad =$$

2. 1250 inch-pounds to meter-kilograms

$$1250 \text{ in.lbs.} \quad X \quad \frac{1 \text{ m}}{39.37 \text{ in.}} \quad X \quad \frac{1 \text{ kg}}{2.205 \text{ lbs.}} \quad =$$

3. 3300 grams per centimeter to pounds per foot

$$\frac{3300 \text{ g}}{\text{cm}} \quad X \quad \frac{1 \text{ lb.}}{453.6 \text{ g}} \quad X \quad \frac{1 \text{ cm}}{0.03281 \text{ ft.}} \quad =$$

4. 25 miles per gallon to kilometers per liter

$$\frac{25 \text{ mi.}}{\text{gal.}} \quad X \quad \frac{1 \text{ km}}{0.6214 \text{ mi.}} \quad X \quad \frac{1 \text{ gal.}}{3.785 \text{ L}} \quad =$$

5. 2850 kilogram meters per minute to pound feet per second

$$\frac{2850 \text{ kg m}}{\text{min.}} \quad X \quad \frac{1 \text{ lb.}}{0.4536 \text{ kg}} \quad X \quad \frac{1 \text{ ft.}}{0.3048 \text{ m}} \quad X \quad \frac{605}{1 \text{ min.}} \quad =$$

6. 50 kilograms per square meter to pounds per acre

$$\frac{50 \text{ kg}}{\text{m}^2} \quad X \quad \frac{1 \text{ lb.}}{0.4536 \text{ kg}} \quad X \quad \frac{4407 \text{ m}^2}{1 \text{ acre}} \quad =$$

Name: _____ Date: _____

Combination Metric Conversions #2

Convert the following problems using the combination conversion method.

1. 318 cubic inches per foot to liters per meter

$$\frac{318 \text{ in}^3}{\text{ft.}} \quad X \quad \frac{1 \text{ L}}{61.03 \text{ in.}^3} \quad X \quad \frac{1 \text{ ft.}}{0.3048 \text{ m}} =$$

2. 8000 feet per minute to centimeters per second

$$\frac{8000 \text{ ft.}}{\text{min.}} \quad X \quad \frac{1 \text{ cm}}{0.03281 \text{ ft.}} \quad X \quad \frac{1 \text{ min.}}{60 \text{ sec.}} =$$

3. 25000 meters per square second to yards per square hour

$$\frac{25000 \text{ m}}{\text{sec.}^2} \quad X \quad \frac{1 \text{ yd.}}{0.9144 \text{ m}} \quad X \quad \frac{3600 \text{ sec.}}{\text{hr.}} \quad X \quad \frac{3600 \text{ sec.}}{\text{hr.}} =$$

4. 0.001 kilograms per day to pounds per minute

$$\frac{0.001 \text{ kg}}{\text{day}} \quad X \quad \frac{1 \text{ lb.}}{0.4536 \text{ kg.}} \quad X \quad \frac{1 \text{ day}}{24 \text{ hr.}} \quad X \quad \frac{1 \text{ hr.}}{60 \text{ min.}} =$$

5. 2 acres per square second to square feet per square second

$$\frac{2 \text{ acre}}{\text{sec.}^2} \quad X \quad \frac{1 \text{ ft.}^2}{0.0000001594 \text{ acre}} =$$

6. 25000 milligrams per millimeter to grams per centimeter

$$\frac{25000 \text{ mg}}{\text{mm}} \quad X \quad \frac{1 \text{ g}}{1000 \text{ mg}} \quad X \quad \frac{10 \text{ mm}}{1 \text{ cm}} =$$

Answer Keys

History of Measurements (page 2)
Discuss these questions in class.

Passus Activity (page 3)
Teacher check

English Measurements (page 4)
1. 220 yd., 660 ft., 33 ropes
2. 5280 yd.
3. 264 ropes
4. 1210 yd.^{2},10890 ft.^{2}, 27.225 ropes^2
5. Teacher check

Volume Activity (page 5)
Teacher check

Hundredweights (page 6)
1. 1093.75 hundredweights, 8750 stones
2. 1225 hundredweights, 4900 quarters

Internet Rodeo #1 (pages 10–11)
1. Argentina, Australia, Austria, Belgium, Brazil, Bulgaria, Cameroon, Canada, Chile, China, Czech Republic, Denmark, Dominican Republic, Egypt, Finland, France, Germany, Hungary, India, Indonesia, Iran, Ireland, Israel, Italy, Japan, Korea (both), Mexico, Netherlands, New Zealand, Pakistan, Poland, Portugal, Romania, Russian Federation, Singapore, Slovakia, South Africa, Spain, Sweden, Switzerland, Thailand, Turkey, United Kingdom, United States, Uruguay, Venezuela
2. "Hard-metric" means measurement, design, and manufacture using the metric system of measurement, but does not include measurement, design, and manufacture using English system measurement units, which are subsequently reexpressed in the metric system of measurement.
3. Teacher check current Board names
4. Net wt. 1 lb. 8 oz. (680 g); Net wt. 1 lb. 8 oz. 680 g; 500 ml (1pt. 0.9 fl. oz.); Net contents 1 gal. 3.79 L
5. It only includes the quantity of food in the container or package; the water or other liquid added is usually included unless specified.
6. Do not use qualifying phrases or terms that exaggerate the amount of food.

Metric Prefix Activity (page 13)
METER:
giga - meter - gigameter - a billion meters - 1,000,000,000 m - 1 Gm
mega - meter - megameter - a million meters - 1,000,000 m - 1Mm
kilo - meter - kilometer - a thousand meters - 1,000 m - 1 km
hecto - meter - hectometer - a hundred meters - 100 m - 1 hm
deca - meter - decameter - ten meters - 10 m - 1 dam
deci - meter - decimeter - a tenth of a meter - 0.1 m - 1 dm
centi - meter - centimeter - a hundredth of a meter - 0.01 m - 1 cm
milli - meter - millimeter - a thousandth of a meter - 0.001 m - 1 mm
micro - meter - micrometer - a millionth of a meter - 0.000001 m - 1 µm
nano - meter - nanometer - a billionth of a meter - 0.000000001 m - 1 nm
FOR GRAM: replace "meter" with "gram" and replace the symbol "m" with the symbol "g"
FOR LITER: replace "meter" with "liter" and replace the "m" with "L or l"

Symbol Identification Activity (page 14)

1. d	5. b	8. b
2. c	6. c, d	9. b, c
3. a, c	7. b	10. d
4. b		

Prefix Challenge Activity (page 16)
1. trillion trillion, billion quadrillion, million quintillion, thousand sextillion
2. billion billionth, million trillionth, thousand quadrillionth
3. billion trillion, million quadrillion, thousand quintillion
4. thousand thousandth

Metric Internet Rodeo #2 (page 17)

1. The quasar PC 1247 + 3406
2. 1.66 yoctograms
3. 1 followed by 100 zeros
4. A quintillion insects, 800,000 species
5. Megagram is a metric ton - 1000 kg, short ton is 2000 pounds, metric ton 2205 pounds, long ton is 2240 pounds
6. It is a computer floating-point arithmetic operation or the rate of speed of a computer that can do one flop per second.
7.

septillion	10^{24}	(24 zeros)
octillion	10^{27}	(27 zeros)
nonillion	10^{30}	(30 zeros)
decillion	10^{33}	(33 zeros)
undecillion	10^{36}	(36 zeros)
duodecillion	10^{39}	(39 zeros)
trecidillion	10^{42}	(42 zeros)
quattuordecillion	10^{45}	(45 zeros)
quindecillion	10^{48}	(48 zeros)
sexdecillion	10^{51}	(51 zeros)
septendecillion	10^{54}	(54 zeros)
octodecillion	10^{57}	(57 zeros)
novemdecillion	10^{60}	(60 zeros)
vigintillion	10^{63}	(63 zeros)

Food and Nutrition Activity (pages 18–19)
Teacher check

Metric Place Value Activity #1 (page 21)

1. 0.001 gram -- 100 meters
2. 1 milligram -- 100,000 millimeters
3. 0.00001 hectogram -- 1 hectometer
4. 0.01decigram -- 1000 decimeters
5. 0.000001 kilogram -- 0.1 kilometers
6. 0.1 centigram -- 10000 centimeters

Metric Place Value Activity #2 (page 22)

1. 1.25 kL
2. 125 daL
3. 1,250,000 mL
4. 398.5 cg
5. 0.003985 kg
6. 39.85 dg

Measurement Activity (pages 23–24)
Teacher check

Body Ruler Activity (page 25)
Teacher check

Reasonable Measurement Activity (page 26)

1. c   2. b   3. b   4. a
5. 0.025 kg
6. 89700 mL
7. 0.000125 km
8. 2,350,000,000 mg
9. 1 m
10. 975 mg
11. 0.000803 kL
12. 0.00004 hg
13. 8.5 dam
14. 0.011 daL
15. 2,235,000 g
16. 0.0105 L
17. b   18. b   19. c

Scientific Number Activity (page 29)

1. 2.9375×10^{18}
2. 5.445×10^{39}
3. 5.77125×10^{14}
4. 1.665×10^{10}
5. 8.165×10^{7}
6. 3.326×10^{5}
7. 2×10^{10}
8. 5.016×10^{9}

Scientific Number Challenge Activity (page 30)

1. 2.226×10^{4}
2. 1.039×10^{4}
3. 5.954×10^{4}
4. 1.12×10^{4}

Electricity Activity (page 31)
Teacher check

Wattage Activity (page 32)
1. 11,520 watts
2. 2,880 watts
3. 3,840 watts
4. 7,680 watts
5. 3,840 watts
6. 5,760 watts

Metric Internet Rodeo #3 (page 33)
1. a. 200 meters
   b. 625 meters
   c. 500 meters - or .5 kilometer
   d. 2.5 kilometers
   e. 10 kilometers
2. a. 59457.9
   b. 1.27
   c. -17.7778°C, 100°C, 86°F, 14°F
   d. 25000.7
   e. 1.13398×10^7
3. a. 27.294 m
   b. 8.5 mm
   c. 14916 km
   d. 2.54 mm

Tool Activity (page 35)

Part 1:	Part 2:
1. 0.125	1. 0.039
2. 0.156	2. 0.079
3. 0.188	3. 0.118
4. 0.219	4. 0.157
5. 0.25	5. 0.197
6. 0.281	6. 0.236
7. 0.313	7. 0.276
8. 0.344	8. 0.315
9. 0.375	9. 0.354
10. 0.406	10. 0.394
11. 0.438	11. 0.433
12. 0.469	12. 0.472
13. 0.5	13. 0.512
14. 0.531	14. 0.551
15. 0.563	15. 0.591
16. 0.594	16. 0.630
17. 0.625	17. 0.669
18. 0.656	18. 0.709
19. 0.688	19. 0.748
20. 0.719	20. 0.787
21. 0.75	21. 0.827
22. 0.781	22. 0.866
23. 0.813	23. 0.906
24. 0.844	24. 0.945

Tool Activity (page 36)
Part 3:

1. 1 mm	25. 1/2
2. 2 mm	26. 13 mm
3. 3 mm	27. 17/32
4. 1/8	28. 14 mm
5. 5/32	29. 9/16
6. 4 mm	30. 15 mm
7. 3/16	31. 19/32
8. 5 mm	32. 5/8
9. 7/32	33. 16 mm
10. 6 mm	34. 21/32
11. 1/4	35. 17 mm
12. 7 mm	36. 11/16
13. 9/32	37. 18 mm
14. 5/16	38. 23/32
15. 8 mm	39. 19 mm
16. 11/32	40. 3/4
17. 9 mm	41. 25/32
18. 3/8	42. 20 mm
19. 10 mm	43. 13/16
20. 13/32	44. 21 mm
21. 11 mm	45. 27/32
22. 7/16	46. 22 mm
23. 15/32	47. 23 mm
24. 12 mm	48. 24 mm

Tonnage Conversion Activity (page 37)
1. 5,292,000 metric tons
2. $79,380,000
3. 5,834,430 U.S. tons
4. $72,930,375
5. Yes, $6,449,625
6. No, because the metric ton is larger than the U.S. standard ton. You will be selling fewer metric tons than you purchased as standard tons.
7. Yes, because the meric ton is larger. You will be selling more standard tons than you purchased as metric tons.

Track and Field Activity (page 40)

1. 109.4 (110)
2. 804.7 (800)
3. 1750.4 (1760)
4. 1236.98
5. 2185.04

6. 301.752 (300)
7. 381
8. 8.82
9. 4.5974
10. 1609.344 (1600)

Conversion Comparison Activity (page 41)

1. 8.2916 ft.^{2}
2. 47.999 ft.^{2}
3. 26.525 m^2
4. 1187.5 cm^2 or 118,750 mm^2

5. 18861.667 ft.
6. 204,600 ft.^{2}
7. 20.82 m or 2082 cm or 20820 mm
8. 32272 m^2

Internet Conversion Calculator Activity (pages 42–43)

Area:

12	0.0012	1.86	0.0129167	2.96526×10^{-7}	4.63323×10^{-10}
15,000	1.5	2325	16.1459	0.0370658	5.79153×10^{-7}
806.45	0.080645	125	0.868056	1.99278×10^{-5}	3.11372×10^{-8}
29032.2	2.90322	4500	31.25	0.00717401	1.12094×10^{-6}
1.01171×10^8	10117.1	1.56816×10^7	108900	2.5	0.0390625
1.48924×10^{10}	1.48924×10^6	2.30833×10^9	1.60301×10^7	368	0.575

Length:

239	2.39	0.00239	94.0945	7.84121	2.61374	0.00148508
152500	1525	1.525	60039.4	5003.28	1667.76	0.947591
1.695×10^6	16950	16.95	667323	55610.2	18536.7	10.5322
62674.5	626.745	0.626745	24675	2056.25	685.417	0.389441
10.668	0.10668	0.00010668	4.2	0.35	0.116607	6.62879×10^{-5}
800.1	8.001	0.008001	315	26.25	8.75	0.00497159
3.78196×10^6	37819.6	37.8196	1.48896×10^{-6}	124080	41360	23.5

Volume:

0.25	2.5×10^{-7}	0.0152559	8.8267×10^{-6}	0.000249993	0.00845345	6.6043×10^{-5}
1.57×10^7	15.7	958073	554.44	15699.6	530877	4147.5
5211.09	0.00521109	318	0.184028	5.21094	176.207	1.37662
998169	0.998169	60912	32.25	998.141	33751.9	263.688
10000.3	0.0100003	610.255	0.353157	10	338.147	2.64179
709.77	0.00070977	43.3128	0.0250653	0.70975	24	0.187501
208198	0.208198	12705	7.35243	208.192	7039.95	55

Weight:

15535	15.535	547.981	34.2488	0.0171244
115550	115.55	4075.91	254.744	0.127372
6995.24	6.99524	246.75	15.4219	0.00771094
1.3134×10^7	13134	463290	28955.6	14.4778
1.1113×10^7	11113	392000	24500	12.25

Fruit:

Didn't anyone ever tell you that you can't compare apples to oranges?

Convert:

1. 2500 cm^3 2. 1235.53 acres   3. 4096.65 mL   4. 248°F   5. 36.7°C

Length Conversion Activity (page 44)

1. 12.9921 in.	9. 2.71272 m
2. 3,408 in.	10. 3218.6 m
3. 4,055,040 in.	11. 290 m
4. 953,541.4 in.	12. 11.494008 m
5. 1,049.5 in.	13. 95,756 m
6. 484 in.	14. 8137.94 m
7. 572,112 in.	15. 77.9145 m
8. 0.098425 in.	16. 23.5966 m

Area Conversion Activity (page 45)

1. 45.327 mi.^{2}
2. 1.882 x 10^{-6} mi.^{2}
3. 3.5714 x 10^{-5} mi.^{2}
4. 3.6954 x 10^{-5} mi.^{2}
5. 9.828 x 10^{-6} mi.^{2}
6. 4.82625 x 10^{-12} mi.^{2}
7. 3.7645 x 10^{-7} mi.^{2}
8. 1.0959 x 10^{-2} mi.^{2}
9. 2.0979 x 10^{12} cm^2
10. 854680 cm^2
11. 2945000 cm^2
12. 5161.6 cm^2
13. 9.10575 x 10^8 cm^2
14. 7560 cm^2
15. 5.5685 x 10^9 cm^2
16. 0.1432344 cm^2

Volume Conversion Activity (page 46)

1. 5.7365 L	9. 4,729.825 in.^{3}
2. 2081.75 L	10. 22.8825 in.^{3}
3. 9.5 L	11. 128,304 in.^{3}
4. 1006.776 L	12. 19,727.4 in.^{3}
5. 2234.16135 L	13. 16,696.25 in.^{3}
6. 97,750 L	14. 1,815,345 in.^{3}
7. 0.0473125 L	15. 98.496 in.^{3}
8. 15.576 L	16. 15.5627 in.^{3}

Weight Conversion Activity (page 47)

1. 25.55 kg	9. 196.189875 lb.
2. 5420.52 kg	10. 511,200 lb.
3. 397.08144 kg	11. 193.543875 lb.
4. 34.9839 kg	12. 5.71875 lb.
5. 21.7728 kg	13. 440 lb.
6. 0.00875 kg	14. 0.01598625 lb.
7. 0.115668 kg	15. 1.65375 lb.
8. 0.0042525 kg	16. 5,312.5 lb.

Temperature Conversion Activity (page 48)

1. 84.2°F
2. 185°F
3. 14°F
4. 62.6°F
5. -148°F
6. 293°F
7. 33.8°F
8. 86°F
9. -1.6°C
10. 29.4°C
11. -23.3°C
12. -8.3°C
13. -73.3°C
14. 62.7°C
15. -17.2°C
16. -1.1°C

If students are using a dual-scale thermometer, the teacher should check their comparisons. Answers found using the formulas are as follows.

17. -3.9°C
18. 86°F
19. -17.8°C
20. 212°F
21. 65.5°C
22. 77°F
23. -1.1°C
24. 32°F
25. 37.8°C
26. 302°F

59

Conversion Practice Activity (page 49)

1. 199.39 cm
2. 1937000 cm
3. 141618.4 cm
4. 0.06096 cm
5. 0.141205 in.^{2}
6. 11734560 in.^{2}
7. 849884700 in.^{2}
8. 1479800.7 in.^{2}
9. 2550 cm^3
10. 45798.5 cm^3
11. 70.8 cm^3
12. 95000 cm^3
13. 47061 g
14. 188244 g
15. 245879.55 g
16. 19765 g
17. -2.5°C
18. 67.2°C
19. -30°C
20. -16.4°C
21. 81.5°F
22. 307.4°F
23. -7.6°F
24. 36.5°F

Combination Metric Conversions Activity #1 (page 53)

1. 1789.598 mph
2. 14.399 mkg
3. 221.735 lb./ft.
4. 10.6293 km/L
5. 1236824.564 lb.ft./sec.
6. 485780.423 lb./acre

Combination Metric Conversions Activity #2 (page 54)

1. 17.1 liters per meter
2. 4063.8 cm per second
3. 3.5433 x 10^{11} yds. per square hour
4. 0.00000153125 pounds per minute
5. 12547051.44 square feet per square second
6. 250 grams per centimeter

Bibliography

Article: *1997 Main Export & Import Goods.* [Online] Available
           http://stats.surfchina.com/glimpse5.html

Article: *A Chronology of the SI Metric System.* [Online] Available
           http://lamar.colostate.edu/~hillger/dates.htm

Article: *A Dictionary of Units.* [Online] Available
           http://www.ex.ac.uk/cimt/dictunit/dictunit.htm

Article: *A Food Labeling Guide: Chapter III - Net Quantity of Contents Statements.* [Online] Available
           http://vm.cfsan.fda.gov/~dms/flg-3.html

Article: *Anglo-Saxon Weights & Measures.* [Online] Available
           http://users.aol.com/JAckProot/met/spvolas.html

Article: *Antoine Frame-of-Reference Method. . .Familiar-Item Examples.* [Online] Available
           http://lamar.colostate.edu/~hillger/fram.htm

Article: *Ask Dr. Math: Metric System Prefixes.* [Online] Available
           http://forum.swarthmore.edu/dr.math/problems/erba9.17.97.html

Article: *Ask Dr. Math: What is the Difference Between a Metric and a Standard Ton?* [Online] Available
           http://forum.swarthmore.edu/dr.math/problems/tondiff.html

Article: *Aunt Edna's Kitchen - Conversion Factors.* [Online] Available
           http://www.cei.net/~terry/auntedna/convert.html

Article: *Build a Solar System.* [Online] Available
           http://www.exploratorium.edu/ronh/solar_system/

Article: *Commonly Used Metric System Units and Symbols.* [Online] Available
           http://lamar.colostate.edu/~hillger/common.htm

Article: *Consumer Products That Come in Metric Sizes.* [Online] Available
           http://lamar.colostate.edu/~hillger/products.htm

Article: *Finding Your Way With Map and Compass.* [Online] Available
           http://info.er.usgs.gov/fact-sheets/finding-your-way.html

Article: *Heat Selection Chart.* [Online] Available
           http://www.cadetco.com/heatchart.html

Article: *History.* [Online] Available
           http://home.clara.net/brianp/history.html

Article: *Improving America.* [Online] Available
           http://www.acq.osd.mil/energylink/metrics/tsld013.htm

Article: *Metrics Matter.* [Online] Available
           http://tqjunior.advancedorg/3804

Article: *Number Names.* [Online] Available
          http://www.hsu.edu/faculty/worthf/googol.html

Article: *Planet Insects.* [Online] Available
          http://www.planetpets.simplenet.com/plntinsc.htm

Article: *Questions and Answers About the Metric System.* [Online] Available
          http://lamar.colostate.edu/~hillger/qanda.htm

Article: *Science Made Simple.* [Online] Available
          http://www.sceincemadesimple.com/~science/Conversion.html

Article: *Sec. 205b. Declaration of Policy.* [Online] Available
          http://www4.law.cornell.edu/uscode/15/205b.text.html

Article: *Sec. 205c. Definitions.* [Online] Available
          http://www4.law.cornell.edu/uscode/15/205c.text.html

Article: *Sec. 205d. Declaration of Policy.* [Online] Available
          http://www4.law.cornell.edu/uscode/15/205d.text.html

Article: *Suggestion to Teachers for a Painless Way to Teach One Facet of SI.* [Online] Available
          http://lamar.colostate.edu/~hillger/teaching.htm

Article: *Symbolic Uses.* [Online] Available
          http://www.newscientist.com/lastword/answers/law78physical.html

Article: *The 48 Member States of the Metre Convention as of 1 August, 1998.* [Online] Available
          http://www.bipm.fr/enus/1_Convention/member_states.html

Article: *The Everyday Metric System* [Online] Available
          http://lamar.colostate.edu/~hillger/everyday.htm

Article: *Tips to Educators for Teaching the Metric System & Ideas for Celebrating National Metric Week,*
          1998 October 4-10. [Online] Available
          http://lamar.colostate.edu/~hillger/week.htm

Article: *Welcome to the Food Pyramid Guide: The Easy Way to Eat Right.* [Online] Available
          http://www.ganesa.com/food/index/html

Article: *Who Uses the Metric System?* [Online] Available
          http://www.acq.osd.mil/energylink/metrics/sld010.htm

Article: *Why Have All the Other Countries Gone Metric?* [Online] Available
          http://www.acq.osd.mil/energylink/metrics/sld007.htm

Article: *Why Should the US Go Metric?* [Online] Available
          http://www.acq.osd.mil/energylink/metrics/sld003.htm